In the evening, leaning over the ba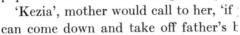
coming, she heard his loud voice in th
into the smoking-room . . . Hasn't the p
they taken it into the kitchen again? Mc
paper's out there – and bring me my sli

'Kezia', mother would call to her, 'if
can come down and take off father's k
would slip down the stairs, holding tightly to the banisters
with one hand – more slowly still, across the hall, and push
open the smoking-room door.

By that time he had his spectacles on and looked at her over
them in a way that was terrifying to the little girl.

'Well, Kezia, get a move on and pull off these boots and
take them outside. Been a good girl today?'

'I d-d-don't know, father.'

'You d-d-don't know? If you stutter like that mother will
have to take you to the doctor.'

She never stuttered with other people – had quite given it
up – but only with father, because then she was trying so hard
to say the words properly.

'What's the matter? What are you looking so wretched
about? Mother, I wish you would teach this child not to appear
on the brink of suicide . . . Here, Kezia, carry my teacup back
to the table – carefully; your hands jog like an old lady's. And
try to keep your handkerchief in your pocket, *not* up your
sleeve.'

'Y-y-es, father.'

On Sundays she sat in the same pew with him in church,
listening while he sang in a loud, clear voice, watching while
he made little notes during the sermon with the stump of a
blue pencil on the back of an envelope – his eyes narrowed to
a slit – one hand beating a silent tattoo on the pew ledge. He
said his prayers so loudly she was certain God heard him above
the clergyman.

He was so big – his hands and his neck, especially his mouth
when he yawned. Thinking about him alone in the nursery was
like thinking about a giant.

On Sunday afternoons grandmother sent her down to the
drawing-room, dressed in her brown velvet, to have a 'nice

Leopards
Edited by Denys Thompson and Christopher Parry

The Little Girl
Katherine Mansfield

The Music Box
Malachi Whitaker

Illustrated by Lynton Lamb

Katherine Mansfield Beauchamp, to give her her full name, was born at Wellington, New Zealand, in 1888. She had part of her education there, and part in London, where she went in 1903. Apart from returning to New Zealand for a couple of years, she spent the rest of her life in Europe, writing stories and, after contracting tuberculosis in 1917, searching for health. Thus much of her work was done under difficulties. Her nature was emotionally restless and her way of life was very emancipated by the standards of the time.

Her first book, *In a German Pension,* appeared in 1911, to be followed by *Prelude* (1916), *Bliss* (1920) and *The Garden Party* (1922). In 1918 she married John Middleton Murry, the critic. She died at Fontainebleau in 1923.

The Little Girl

KATHERINE MANSFIELD

To the little girl he was a figure to be feared and avoided. Every morning before going to business he came into the nursery and gave her a perfunctory kiss, to which she responded with 'Goodbye, father'. And oh, the glad sense of relief when she heard the noise of the buggy growing fainter and fainter down the long road!

talk with father and mother'. But the little girl always found mother reading *The Sketch* and father stretched out on the couch, his handkerchief on his face, his feet propped on one of the best sofa pillows, and so soundly sleeping that he snored.

She, perched on the piano-stool, gravely watched him until he woke and stretched, and asked the time – then looked at her.

'Don't stare so, Kezia. You look like a little brown owl.'

One day, when she was kept indoors with a cold, the grandmother told her that father's birthday was next week, and suggested she should make him a pin-cushion for a present out of a beautiful piece of yellow silk.

Laboriously, with a double cotton, the little girl stitched three sides. But what to fill it with? That was the question. The grandmother was out in the garden, and she wandered into mother's bedroom to look for 'scraps'. On the bed-table she discovered a great many sheets of fine paper, gathered them up, shredded them into tiny pieces, and stuffed her case, then sewed up the fourth side.

That night there was a hue and cry over the house. Father's great speech for the Port Authority had been lost. Rooms were ransacked – servants questioned. Finally mother came into the nursery.

'Kezia, I suppose you didn't see some papers on a table in our room?'

'Oh yes', she said. 'I tore them up for my s'prise.'

'*What!*' screamed mother. 'Come straight down to the dining-room this instant.'

And she was dragged down to where father was pacing to and fro, hands behind his back.

'Well?' he said sharply.

Mother explained.

He stopped and stared in a stupefied manner at the child.

'Did you do that?'

'N-n-no', she whispered.

'Mother, go up to the nursery and fetch down the damned thing – see that the child's put to bed this instant.'

Crying too much to explain, she lay in the shadowed room

watching the evening light sift through the venetian blinds and trace a sad little pattern on the floor.

Then father came into the room with a ruler in his hands.

'I am going to whip you for this', he said.

'Oh, no, no!' she screamed, cowering down under the bed-clothes.

He pulled them aside.

'Sit up', he commanded, 'and hold out your hands. You must be taught once and for all not to touch what does not belong to you.'

'But it was for your b-b-birthday.'

Down came the ruler on her little, pink palms.

Hours later, when the grandmother had wrapped her in a shawl and rocked her in the rocking-chair, the child cuddled close to her soft body.

'What did Jesus make fathers for?' she sobbed.

'Here's a clean hanky, darling, with some of my lavender water on it. Go to sleep, pet; you'll forget all about it in the morning. I tried to explain to father, but he was too upset to listen tonight.'

But the child never forgot. Next time she saw him she whipped both hands behind her back, and a red colour flew into her cheeks.

The Macdonalds lived in the next-door house. Five children there were. Looking through a hole in the vegetable garden fence the little girl saw them playing 'tag' in the evening. The father with the baby Mac on his shoulders, two little girls hanging on to his coat tails, ran round and round the flower-beds, shaking with laughter. Once she saw the boys turn the hose on him – *turn the hose on him* – and he made a great grab at them, tickling them until they got hiccoughs.

Then it was she decided there were different sorts of fathers.

Suddenly, one day, mother became ill, and she and grand-mother drove into town in a closed carriage.

The little girl was left alone in the house with Alice, the 'general'. That was all right in the daytime, but while Alice was putting her to bed she grew suddenly afraid.

'What'll I do if I have nightmare?' she asked. 'I *often* have nightmare, and then grannie takes me into her bed – I can't stay in the dark – it all gets "whispery". . . . What'll I do if I do?'

'You just go to sleep, child', said Alice, pulling off her socks and whacking them against the bedrail, 'and don't you holler out and wake your poor pa.'

But the same old nightmare came – the butcher with a knife and a rope who grew nearer and nearer, smiling that dreadful smile, while she could not move, could only stand still, crying out, 'Grandma, Grandma!' She woke shivering, to see father beside her bed, a candle in his hand.

'What's the matter?' he said.

'Oh, a butcher – a knife – I want grannie.' He blew out the candle, bent down and caught up the child in his arms, carrying her along the passage to the big bedroom. A newspaper was on the bed – a half-smoked cigar balanced against his reading-lamp. He pitched the paper on the floor, threw the cigar into the fire-place, then carefully tucked up the child. He lay down beside her. Half asleep still, still with the butcher's smile all about her, it seemed she crept close to him, snuggled her head under his arm, held tightly to his pyjama jacket.

Then the dark did not matter; she lay still.

'Here, rub your feet against my legs and get them warm', said father.

Tired out, he slept before the little girl. A funny feeling came over her. Poor father! Not so big, after all – and with no one to look after him . . . He was harder than the grandmother, but it was a nice hardness . . . And every day he had to work and was too tired to be a Mr Macdonald . . . She had torn up all his beautiful writing . . . She stirred suddenly, and sighed.

'What's the matter?' asked father. 'Another dream?'

'Oh', said the little girl, 'my head's on your heart; I can hear it going. What a big heart you've got, father dear.'

Malachi Whitaker was born in 1895 at Bradford in Yorkshire, and went to school there. Her son and daughter and seven grandchildren have all done well at school, and on this she comments, 'This seems to me a good record, as I disliked school intensely, never listened to anything, but lived a complete life of my own and emerged with a soul of my own, thank heaven. But no education . . .' And of her stories Mrs Whitaker says, 'Why I began to write out of the blue when I was 33, I don't know. I had no aims. Why I stopped, I don't know either. I was compelled to write what I had been thinking for over thirty years. What most deeply touched me in the earlier days was the injustice invariably dealt out to the inarticulate.'

Mrs Whitaker now lives at Ash in Kent, where she 'reads a lot, and walks a lot'.

The Music Box

MALACHI WHITAKER

A woman and a little boy were walking down the steep, cobbled street of a village. The woman was young. She was short, only about five feet in height, and she had small feet, of which she was very proud. The little boy had large, hazel eyes, both timid and thoughtful. He held his mother's hand. The two of them had the same expression of joyous solemnity; they were going to buy something.

The husband of the woman was called Theakstone Morphett. He was older than his wife, and worked in a stone quarry as a trimmer. He was a big-built man, without very much flesh, and he had a harsh, growling voice which frightened his son.

His wife had never been able to call him by his Christian name, Theakstone. It seemed to her silly, so she called him 'the father'..

The boy Henry could not quite make up his mind about 't'father'. The house was certainly better and quieter without this man, who sprawled in the high-backed wooden chair that

8

had the goatskin tied over the top of it, and looked discontentedly at his small son; who often let it be known that he would have preferred a big, fat, rollicking, sandy baby to this quiet creature with questioning eyes.

Henry could not bear to be far away from his mother; she was the only real part of his world. There were other children of the same age living near, but he did not feel the want of a playmate. Each Sunday his mother would take him to the tiny stone chapel, where they sat on plain, wooden forms, which had lengths of red baize upon them. The forms were slippery, and sometimes the baize would writhe noiselessly to the floor.

Everything at the chapel was delightful. But the best thing of all was the music.

A harmonium was all they could afford at the chapel, and an elderly, very kind-faced woman played it. She sat with her back to the congregation, because she had no self-consciousness at all. She would slip on to the round stool in front of it, the gathers of her thick and proper skirt oozing gently over the edges; her feet would press firmly on the pedals, she would work them once or twice to fill the bellows with air, then the music would come.

The boy and his mother loved it. They sang the hymns loudly. There was one they often had. 'Toiling on', they would sing, and the harmonium seemed to add, 'Ha, ha, ha! Toiling on! Ha, ha, ha!' It was worth coming to hear, however wet the day.

Once there had been a tea at the chapel, and they had both gone. The wooden forms were now arranged round long trestle tables. Plates of potted meat sandwiches, buns, biscuits and sweet cakes stood above the short or long, old or new table-cloths that had been lent.

There was a small cloakroom just inside the chapel, and on the day of the tea, the precious harmonium had been moved into this place to give more room in the main hall. Here the boy found it. Furtively he tried the lid. It was open. His heart beat quickly as he put his hand on the soft-falling ivory keys. How pleasant they felt. He pulled up the chair with a back – the one used for reaching up to the cloakroom light – and sat down to play the silent keys.

Soon he got tired of this, and began to press the pedals. As he heard the rushing sound of the air, he touched a note. He became a little bolder, and suddenly a tune played under his hand –'Toiling on! Ha, ha, ha!' He was frightened and happy, though however hard he tried he could not get past the first line.

'Music!' he whispered: then he jumped up and went to look for his mother.

She was helping to wash up. He stood beside her, tugging at her skirt.

He waited until they were in the main hall, with its chattering crowd. Then he said, 'Come and listen to me play the harmonium!'

Guiltily they stole into the cloakroom and closed the door. The boy had a pink colour in his face, he was excited.

'Listen!' he cried.

He pressed down his feet and played his tune with confidence. Over and over again he played the first line of 'Toiling on!'

'Wait a minute!' she cried, 'try this for the second line.'

Between them, miraculously, they found it. How happy they were. The noise grew louder, and their joy with it. When the door opened, and Miss Altass – the-playing lady – came in, there they froze into a picture of guilt, one sitting, the other half-standing.

'You mustn't touch the harmonium', said Miss Altass, not so gently as usual. She closed and locked it. They watched her, and did not say a word, only moved quietly away.

But afterwards, at home, they had something new to talk about. They could recall the scene a hundred times, and never tire. And one day, the little boy said dreamily, 'I wish we had some music.'

His mother had just taken the last loaf from the oven, and placed it on end on the baking-board. She pushed the warm oven-cloth under her chin and stood there thinking. The little boy looked at her, and smiled because she was smiling. Gradually, her face grew bleak; she said, 'T'father 'ud never let us 'ave any in the 'ouse. 'E doesn't like it.'

10

After that, she had cheered up, and between them, they made a secret. She was going to save up for a harmonium, and then they would go and buy one. It would be hard to save, because there was never much money; but she could try. Penny by penny, a little hoard grew.

At last, the mother got the greengrocer, who called every Thursday, to change her pennies into shillings for her. There were not many, but she thought, 'We might get an old one, that didn't cost much, and I would pay a bit every time I could save it.'

It was a mild, dull afternoon in early autumn when they walked down the street. Mrs Morphett held in one hand a purse, containing her money, and the advertisement which she had cut out of the paper. It read, 'Musical instruments of all descriptions for sale. Unlimited choice. Apply 13 St Leonard's Terrace.'

At last they arrived at St Leonard's Terrace. They opened the gate of thirteen, and walked up to the house entrance and knocked.

In front of them was a large door, with a great amber-coloured knob on it. Henry stared at the knob, and thought it was so beautiful that for one moment he almost forgot the object of the visit. A tall, thin man with a black moustache answered their knock.

'Come forward', said the man, speaking in a deep, rich voice. They went forward only as far as the square hall, and stopped. 'Follow me', he continued, still in the same deep tones, and they followed him down the passage into a dark back room, amid a profusion of fiddles, harps, pianos, and all shapes and sizes of musical instruments.

The little boy felt very proud of his mother as she looked up into the face of the dark gentleman and said, 'How much is the harmonium?' She even managed to smile, a small, terrified smile. He thought she looked very pretty.

As soon as she heard the price, she turned and made for the door, pulling the reluctant child with her; but before they could reach it, somehow the dark gentleman was in their way. He began to smile and talk to them, he did not want them to go without buying something. He showed them a square

yellow box, covered with painted red flowers. 'This', he said, 'might be something more in your line?'

As he spoke, he lifted the box on to an old packing-case, pushed into it a roll of perforated paper, and began to turn a handle. The boy and woman stood as stiff as statues, but entranced. Besides this, a harmonium was nothing! The first tinkling tune it played was 'The Minstrel Boy', which Mrs Morphett had learned long ago at school. She nodded her head and began to hum, her eyes shining.

'What is it, mother?' whispered the little boy.

'It's a music-box', said his mother, 'and if it isn't too dear, we'll buy it.'

She imagined it playing for ever in the kitchen at home. They would put it on the end of the dresser, and treat it so carefully.

The man, who had been considering a price, smoothed down his moustache.

'You can have it for six shillings', he said, 'and the tunes alone are worth that.'

The mother and son looked at each other, he hopefully, she happily, then they both looked at the dark gentleman. And a few minutes afterwards they passed again the iron railings of numbers eleven, nine, seven, five, three, and one, the woman carrying a large box, inadequately wrapped, as if it were a holy thing.

They seemed to reach home in a moment. How well the box fitted its corner of the dresser, how the red flowers on its lid winked in the firelight! They played several tunes before they took off their outdoor things. His mother turned the handle while the little boy sat on his chair looking at her with solemn, ecstatic eyes. They were both serious, grave, and spoke little. Once, the mother said in a sharp, defiant voice, 'You sh'll 'ave an 'armonium next year', although she knew it was next to impossible. The harmonium did not seem to matter so much now.

All at once they heard footsteps.

'It's t'father!' said the boy, in dismay. There was no meal ready for him.

They jumped up and ran to the door, looking like two

children, flushed and happy. The little boy boldly took hold of one yellow trouser leg and cried, 'Father, father!' The man said, 'Wheer's my tea?'

'It won't be a minute.' His wife pushed the kettle into the heart of the fire and hurriedly put some things on the table.

The father seemed to be annoyed about something. He had lost a shilling that afternoon. It was not often that he put money on a horse, and, almost without exception, he lost. But he never gave up hoping that next time it would come off at a long price. All at once his glance fell on the music-box.

'What's that contraption?' he growled.

Looking at him, the little boy began to whimper. It came over him that his father was possessed of power, and that he would use it cruelly. The mother seemed to feel that way too. Shading her face with the teapot, she stood waiting for the kettle to boil. She had the look of a child waiting to be whipped.

'Come on, let's be knowin'. What's that contraption?' He was proud of the long word.

'It – it's a music-box,' she said, almost inaudibly.

He looked at it dully.

The little boy watched his father's face. Then, still whimpering, he dragged a stool to the edge of the dresser, stood up on it, and began to turn the handle.

The man listened for a minute, then a heavy anger settled on his face. 'Shut that row!' he shouted, standing up and waving his arms. ' 'Oo brought that blasted thing into the 'ouse?'

The little boy stopped turning, and as he looked at the father, the bright colour ran out of his face, leaving only a sickly pallor around his two staring dark eyes. The lid of the kettle began to shake, but the mother did not pour the boiling water into the teapot.

'Well, you can tek it back', said the man. He kept looking at the box indignantly, as if it had done him some injury.

The water from the kettle began to splash on to the fire, and that was the only sound to be heard in the room.

As soon as the man had set off to his work the next morning, the woman slowly dressed to go out. She buttoned the boy into his overcoat, and opened the door. There was a fog, and they both coughed as they stepped out into the street. They had not been able to eat any breakfast, and they shivered in the chill morning air. The woman carried the music-box, wrapped and ready to go back. She had cried until she was weary, and so had the little boy. They had asked again to be allowed to keep the music-box, had promised that it shouldn't be played when t'father was in, but he simply said, 'Tek it back.' He could not see why his wife and son should want music when he did not.

The two walked very slowly, as the box seemed heavy. The mother was ashamed. She did not know how to approach the tall, dark gentleman; she was afraid he would not give her her money back. There was only one bright spot. She had not told her husband that the thing was paid for. Indeed, she had not had the chance, and the boy had clung to her dress, quietly, all the time her husband had shouted.

At last, once more, they were in St Leonard's Terrace. The tall houses were wrapped in fog, water dripped from the trees with their few twisted leaves, and the pavements were so greasy that many times they slipped and almost fell.

As his mother timidly knocked at the door, the little boy wiped the moisture from the amber-coloured knob, so that he could better see it. In doing so, he turned it, and the door opened softly beneath his hand. There was not a sound to be heard. He turned to his mother, looking up at her humbly, out of his swollen eyes. She seemed to understand him. Pushing open the door with her arm, she carefully lowered the parcel on to the floor of the little square hall, then she gently closed the door. Very soon the two figures had vanished in the fog . . .

'The Little Girl' from *Collected Stories* by Katherine Mansfield
is reprinted by permission of The Society of Authors. © The
Estate of Katherine Mansfield 1912. 'The Music Box' from
Frost in April by Malachi Whitaker is reprinted by permission
of the author. © Malachi Whitaker 1929. Notes, illustrations
and design © Cambridge University Press 1972.

ISBNs:
0 521 08332 X the pamphlet
0 521 08378 8 Series B

Cambridge University Press
Printed in Great Britain by
Ebenezer Baylis & Son Ltd
Leicester and London